ENCHANTING ORIGAMI

Fabulous Fashion ORIGAMI

JOE FULLMAN

WINDMILL BOOKS

Published in 2021 by Windmill Books,
an Imprint of Rosen Publishing
29 East 21st Street, New York, NY 10010

Cataloging-in-Publication Data

Names: Fullman, Joe.
Title: Fabulous fashion origami / Joe Fullman.
Description: New York : Windmill Books, 2021. | Series: Enchanting origami | Includes glossary and index.
Identifiers: ISBN 9781499485417 (pbk.) | ISBN 9781499485431 (library bound) | ISBN 9781499485424 (6 pack) | ISBN 9781499485448 (ebook)
Subjects: LCSH: Origami--Juvenile literature. | Fashion in art--Juvenile literature.
Classification: LCC TT872.5 F85 2021 | DDC 736'.982--dc23

Manufactured in the United States of America

CPSIA Compliance Information: Batch BS20WM: For Further Information contact Rosen Publishing, New York, New York at 1-800-237-9932

Contents

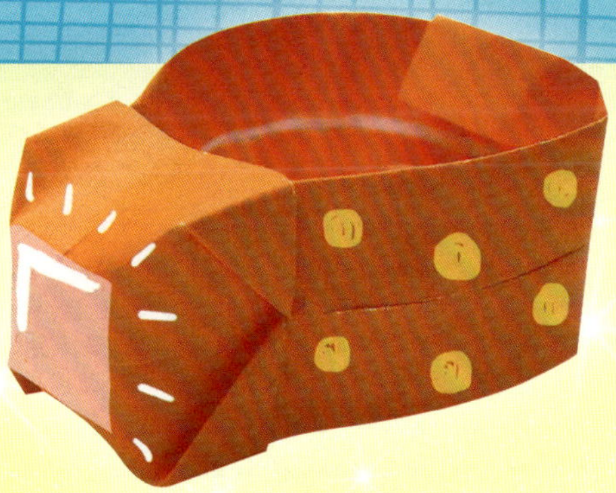

Introduction

Let's explore the wonderful world of enchanted origami. In this book, you'll learn how to make some magical fashion jewelry, including a unicorn brooch, an enchanted crown, a giant jewel, and a magic bracelet.

In traditional origami, the models are usually made from a single sheet of folded paper with no cutting or gluing involved. We've broken the rules here and there to make our models as magical as possible.

Ask an adult to help with any projects that need scissors and glue. Otherwise, all you need to get started is a square of paper and your fingers. If you haven't made origami models before, try some of the easy projects first. Now, let's get ready for some fantastic folding!

Getting Started

The paper used in origami is thin but strong, so that it can be folded many times. You can use ordinary scrap paper, as long as it's not too thick.

A lot of these origami models are made with the same folds and basic starting designs, known as "bases." This introduction explains some of the ones that will appear most, so it's a good idea to master these before you start. When making the projects, follow the key to find out what the lines and arrows mean. And always crease well!

Key

- Valley fold
- Mountain fold
- Step fold
- Direction to move paper
- Push/flatten
- Rotate by x degrees
- Cut with scissors
- Glue
- Turn paper over

Basic Folds

Valley Fold

To make a valley fold, fold the edges of the paper toward you, so that the crease is pointing down, like a valley.

Mountain Fold

To make a mountain fold, fold the edges of the paper away from you, so that the crease is pointing up, like a mountain.

Step Fold

A step fold is used to make a step or zigzag in the paper.

1. Valley fold the paper in half. Then make a mountain fold directly above the valley fold.

2. Push the mountain fold over the valley fold and press down flat.

3. You now have a step fold. You can also make it in reverse, with the mountain fold first.

Reverse Folds

Inside Reverse Fold

This is useful if you want to flatten part of an origami model. It's a good way to create shapes for your jewelry.

1

Fold a piece of paper diagonally in half, as shown. Make a valley fold on one point and crease.

2

It's important to make sure that the paper is creased well. Run your finger over the crease two or three times.

3

Unfold, and then turn the crease you've just made into a mountain fold. Unfold, and open up the corner slightly.

4

Open up the paper a little more and then tuck the tip of the point inside. Close the paper. This is the view from the underside of the paper.

5

Flatten the paper. You now have an inside reverse fold.

Outside Reverse Fold

This is great if you want to make part of your model stick out. It will come in handy for making heads and tails.

1

Fold a piece of paper diagonally in half, as shown. Make a valley fold on one point and crease.

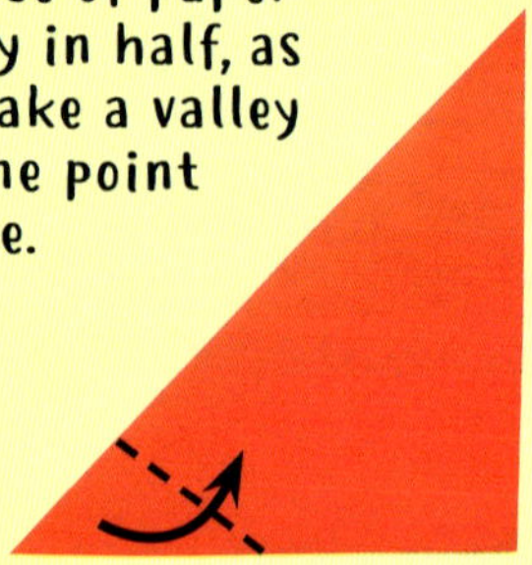

2

It's important to make sure that the paper is creased well. Run your finger over the crease two or three times.

3

Unfold, and then turn the crease you've just made into a mountain fold. Unfold, and open up the corner slightly.

4

Open up the paper a little more and start to turn the corner inside out. Then close the paper when the fold begins to turn.

5

Flatten the paper. You now have an outside reverse fold.

Kite Base

1

Place your paper like this. Valley fold it in half from left to right.

2

Valley fold the left-hand point over to the middle crease.

3

Repeat step 2 on the other side.

4

You now have a kite base.

Unicorn Brooch

How would you like to wear your very own unicorn? You'll need a safety pin to complete this project.

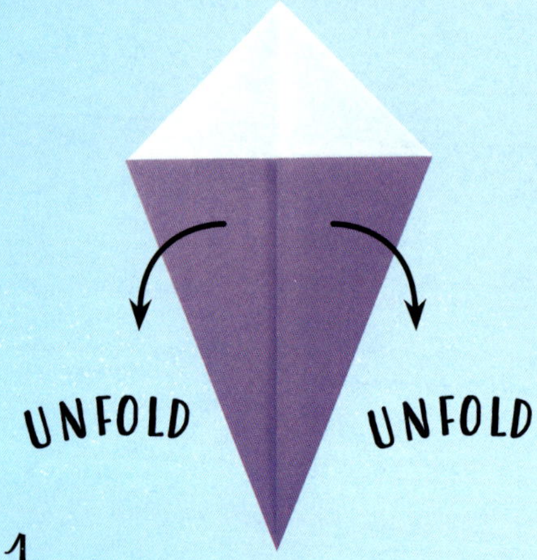

1
Start with a kite base (see page 7) placed this way up. Unfold the left- and right-hand sides.

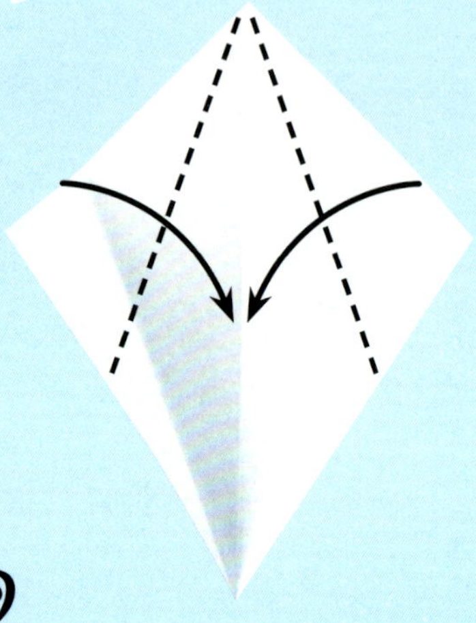

2
Make a kite base the other way up by folding the top left and the top right edges over to the central line.

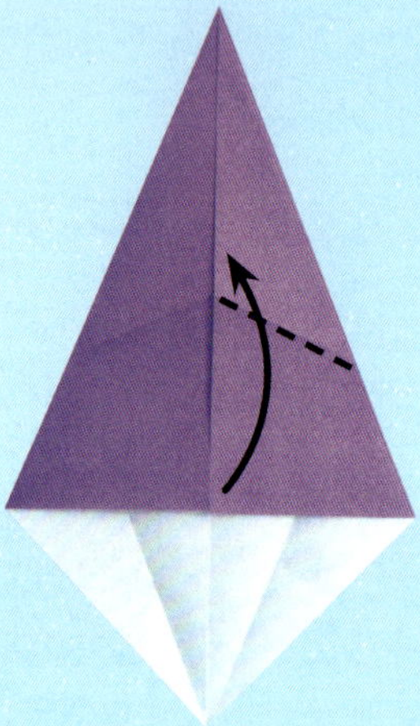

3
Make a valley fold along the crease, as shown. As you do, lift the bottom left point of the right-hand flap and bring it up in line with the central crease.

4
As you bring the point up, the right-hand side of the paper should fold over to the middle, creating a new flap. Flatten the paper down.

5
Your paper should look like this with a straight horizontal edge at the top of the new flap. Repeat steps 3 and 4 on the left-hand side.

6
Turn your paper over from left to right.

Hard

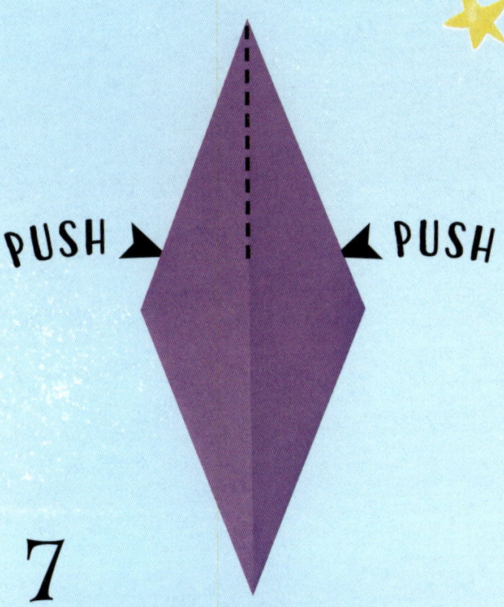

7
Push together the sides at the top, forming a new valley fold and bringing the top point forward toward you.

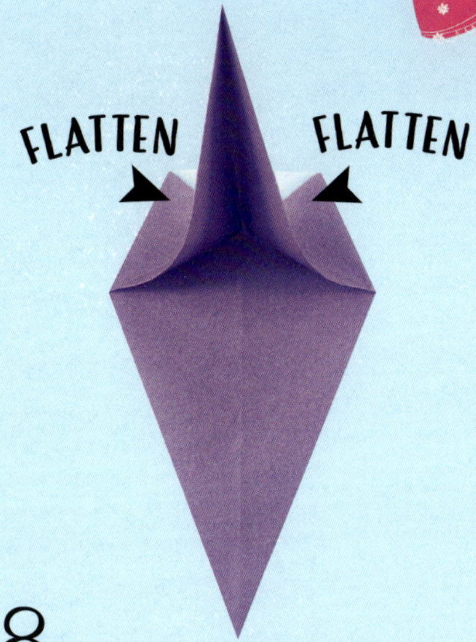

8
Push the sides of the pointed flap together and flatten the paper, so the flap is pointing toward you.

9
Open up the sides of the pointed flap from underneath, and gently pull apart so the point starts to flatten.

10
Now push down on top of the flap, squashing it down onto the paper to form a triangle shape.

11
Your paper should look like this. Turn it over from left to right.

12
Rotate the paper 180°.

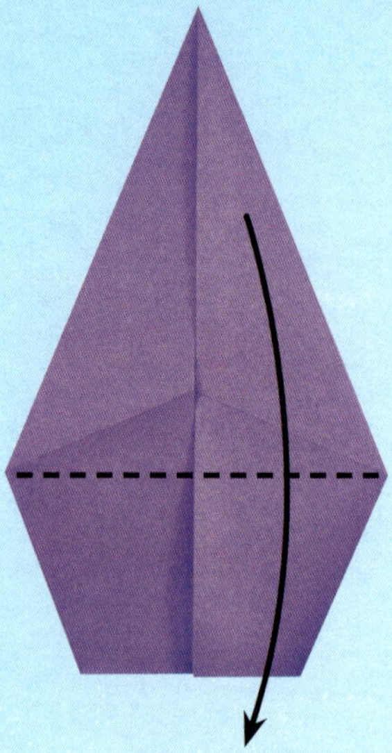

13

Valley fold the top point down, as shown.

14

Turn the paper over from left to right.

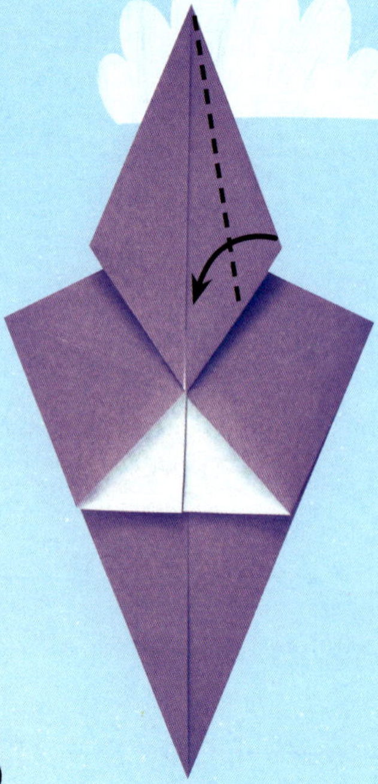

15

Make a small valley fold at the top on the right-hand side, as shown, so the right edge meets the central crease.

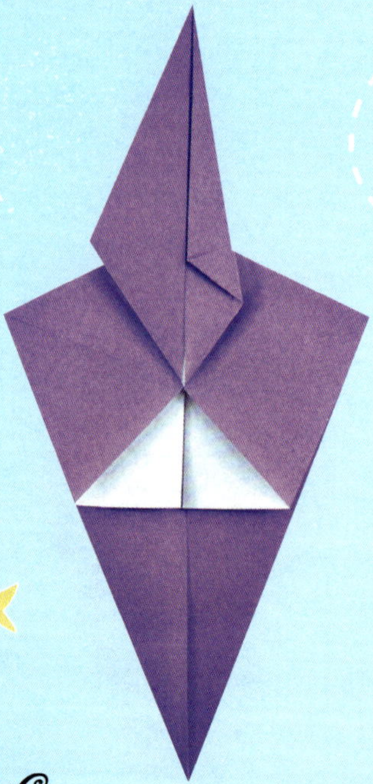

16

Repeat step 15 on the left-hand side.

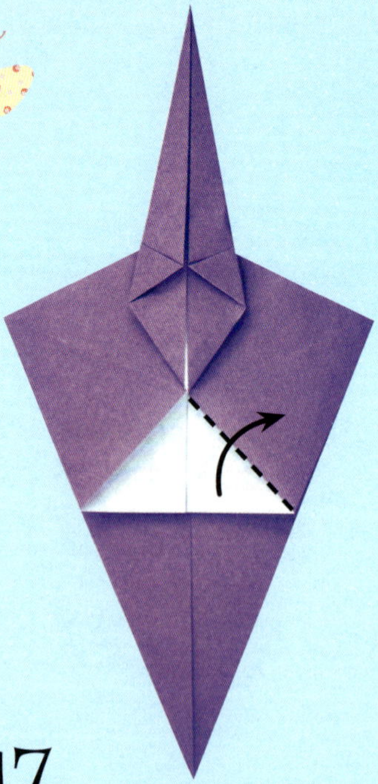

17

Valley fold the white triangle on the right-hand side.

18

Repeat step 17 on the left-hand side.

Hard

19

Unfold the folds you made in steps 17 and 18.

20

Tuck the white triangle on the right-hand side under the flap above it.

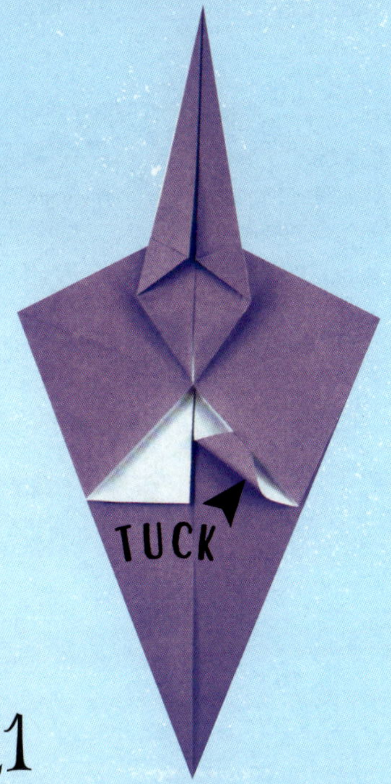

21

Make sure the triangle goes all the way in.

22

Repeat steps 20 and 21 on the left-hand side.

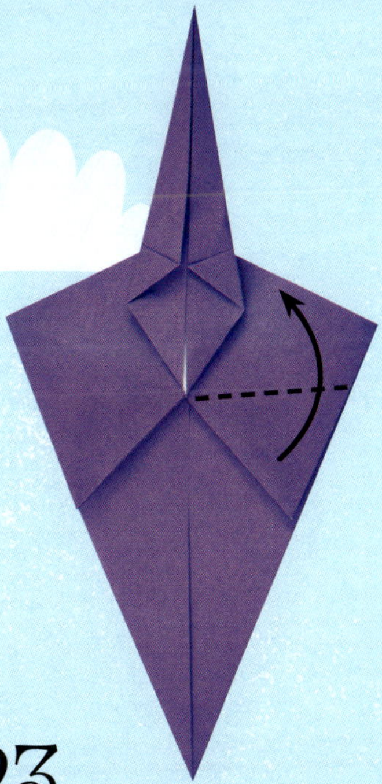

23

Valley fold the upper right-hand flap, as shown, so that the point overlaps the top edge. This is one of your unicorn's ears.

24

Repeat step 23 on the left-hand side.

25
Turn the paper over from left to right.

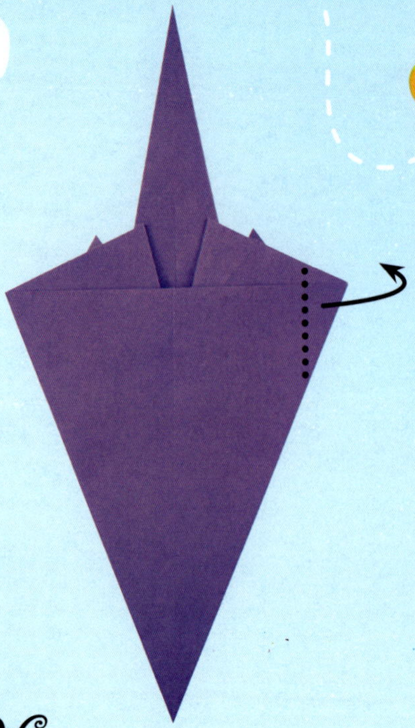

26
Mountain fold the right-hand point, as shown.

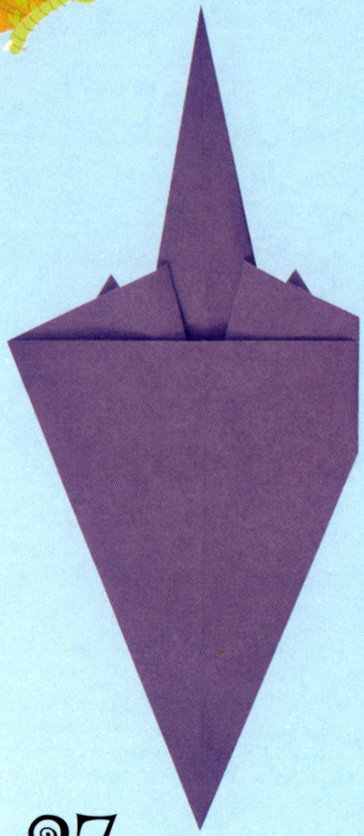

27
Repeat step 26 on the left-hand side.

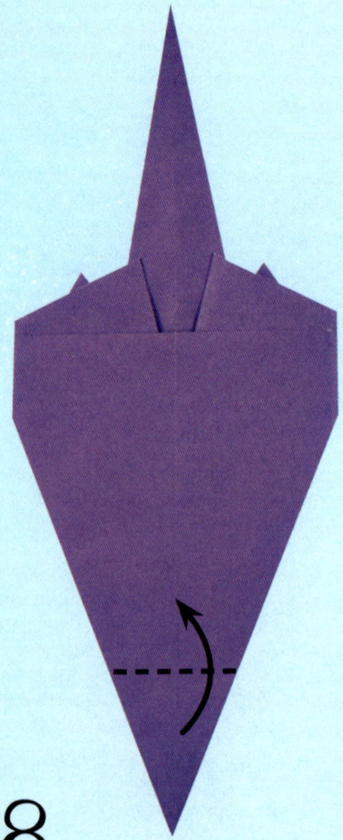

28
Valley fold the bottom point, as shown.

29
Turn the paper over from left to right.

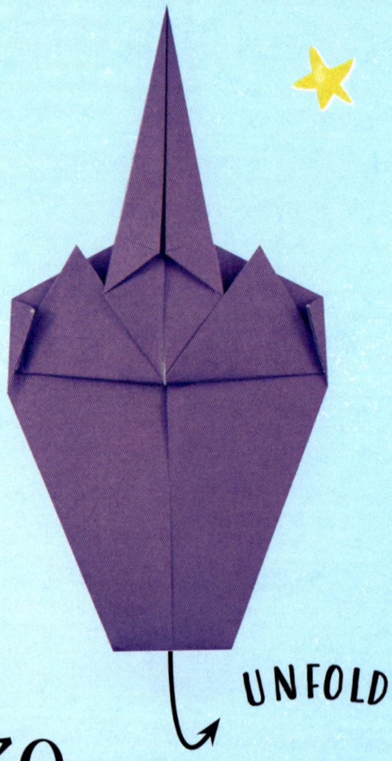

30
Unfold the fold you made in step 28, bringing the point down to the bottom.

Hard

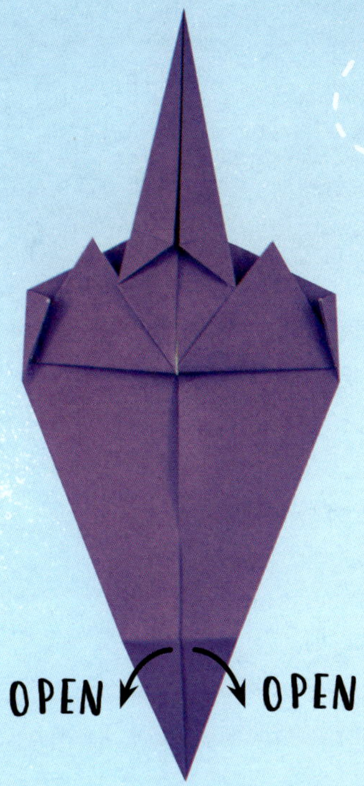

31
Open up the flaps at the bottom, just above the point.

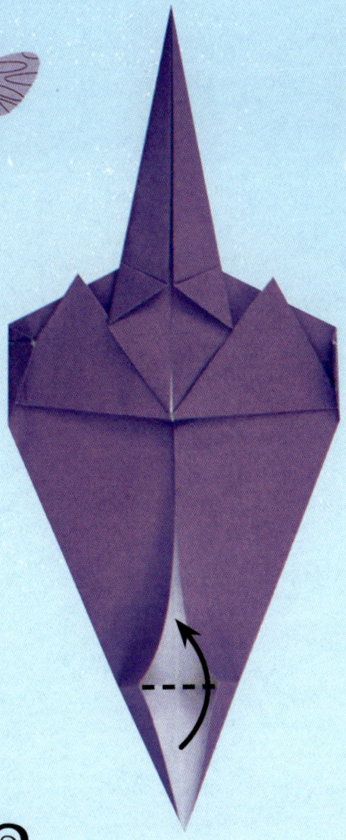

32
Lift the point up and tuck it under the flaps you opened in step 31.

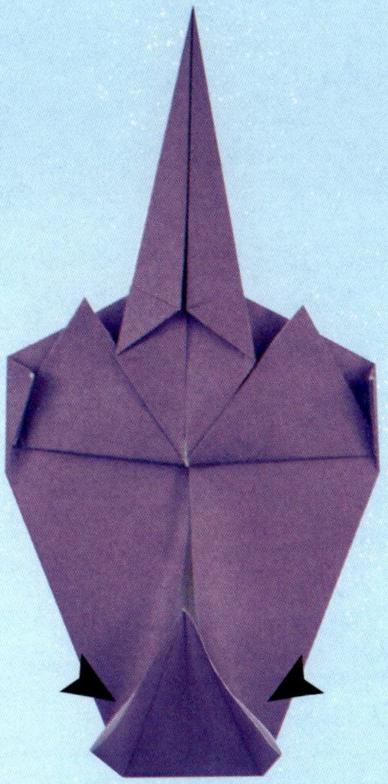

33
Flatten down the flaps on both sides over the point.

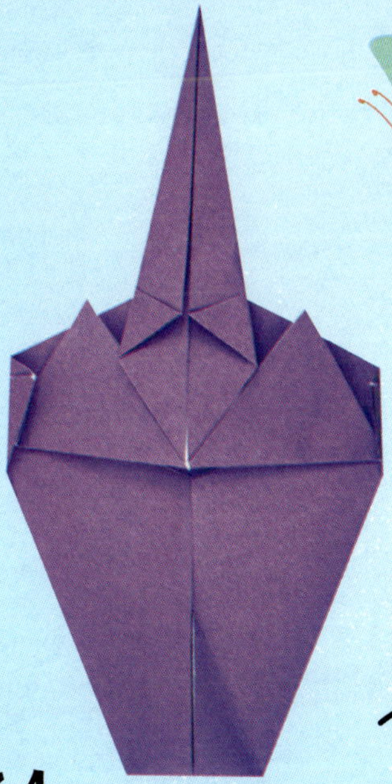

TURN OVER

34
Your paper should look like this. Ask a grown-up to fix a safety pin to this side of the paper, then turn it over from left to right. Decorate your pin!

Enchanted Crown

Here's a crown fit for a unicorn—the royalty of the forest. It's also big enough for you to wear! You will need six pieces of paper for this project.

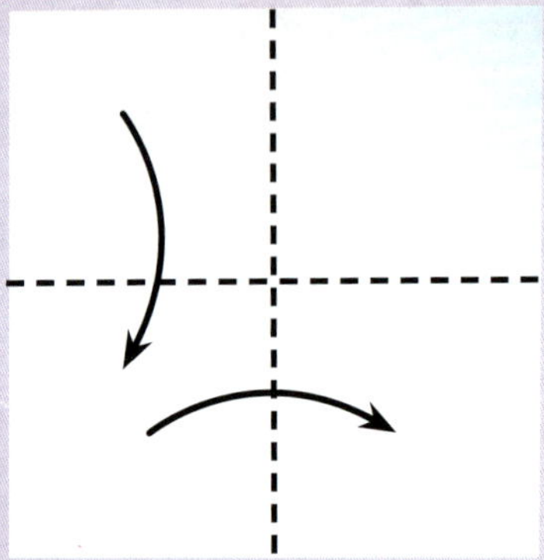

1

Place your first piece of paper like this, white side up with a straight edge facing you. Fold it in half from left to right, and unfold. Then fold it in half from top to bottom, and unfold.

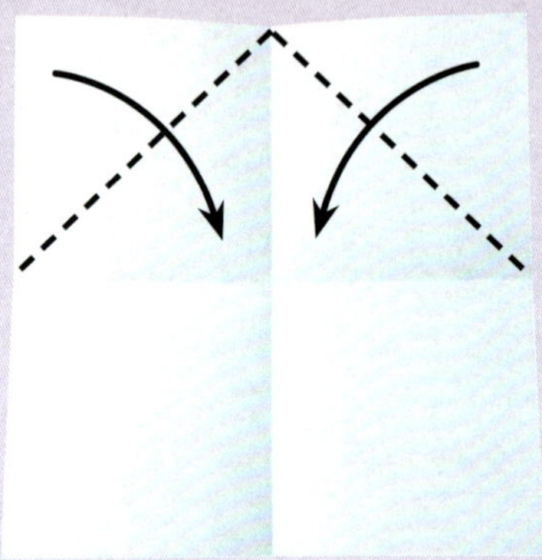

2

Fold the top left and the top right corners down to the central point.

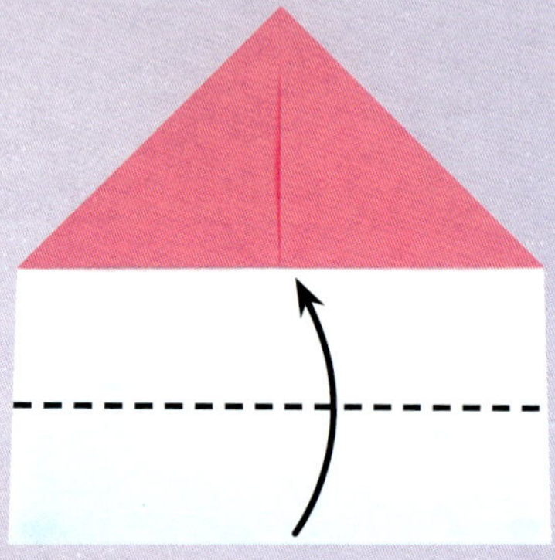

3

Fold the bottom edge up so it meets the bottom edge of the two triangular flaps.

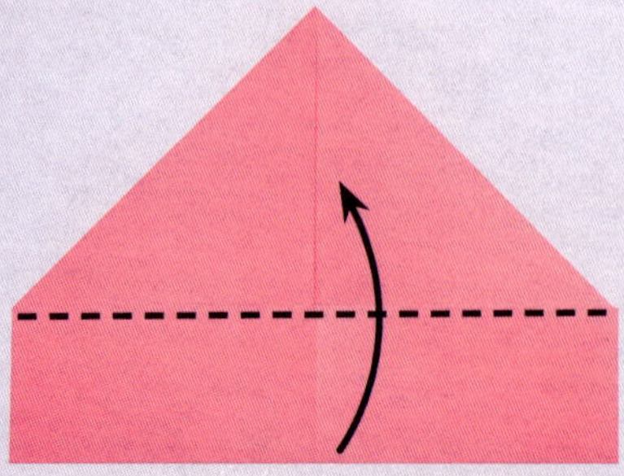

4

Fold the bottom edge up again along the line formed by the bottom edge of the two triangular flaps.

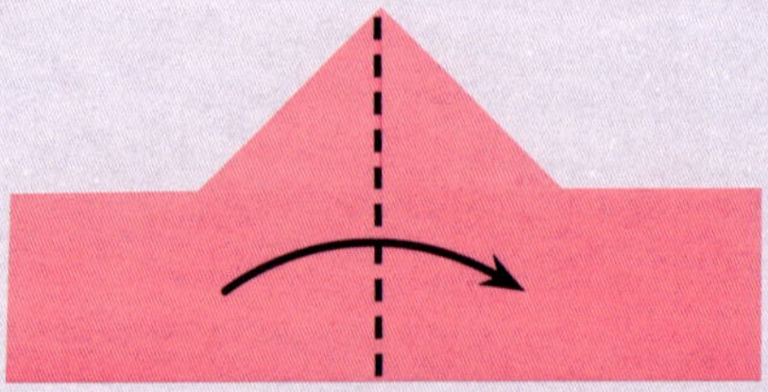

5

Fold the paper in half from left to right.

6

Unfold the folds you made in steps 4 and 5.

Easy

7

Your paper should look like this. Repeat steps 1 to 6 with your other pieces of paper.

8

Take your first piece of paper and slide its right-hand bottom edge inside the bottom flap of the second piece of paper. Keep pushing until it's about halfway across.

9

Your paper should look like this.

10

Now slide the right-hand bottom edge of the second piece of paper inside the bottom flap of the third piece of paper. Keep pushing until it's about halfway across.

11

Your paper should like this. Keep repeating steps 8 to 10 until all six pieces of paper are joined together.

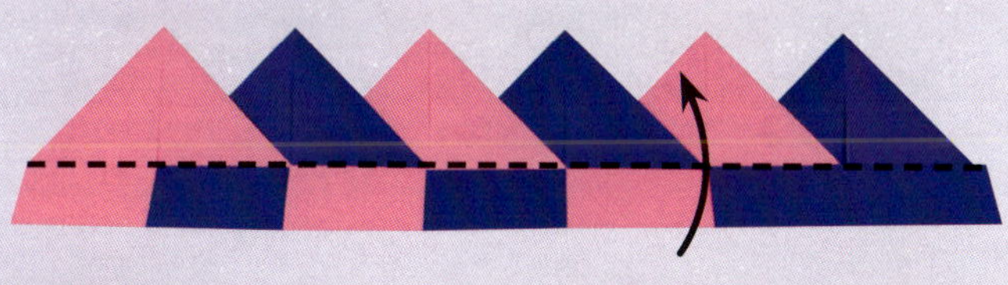

12

Fold over the bottom edge of all six pieces of paper at once, which will hold the pieces together.

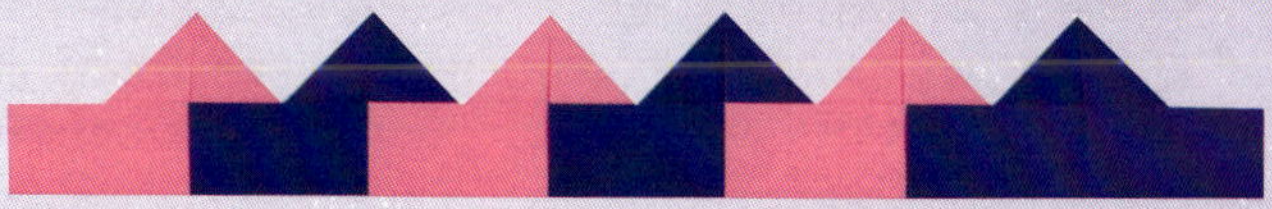

13

Lift the six-piece model up and begin folding it around into a circle shape.

14

Slot one end into the other, just like you did with all the other pieces of paper.

15

It's time to decorate your crown with jewels and precious gems. Maybe you could stick a magic gem to the front (see pages 16–19)?

Giant Jewel

All unicorns like shiny precious gems, particularly ones as big and as full of magic as this one. You'll need three pieces of paper to complete this giant jewel.

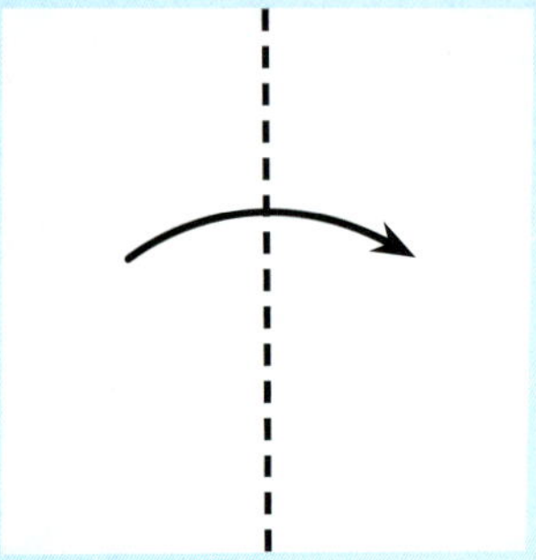

1

Take your first piece of paper and place it like this, white side up, with a straight edge facing you. Valley fold it in half from left to right, then unfold.

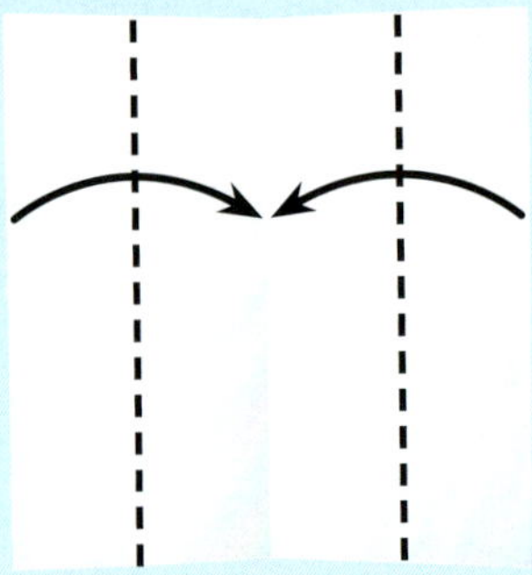

2

Valley fold the left- and right-hand edges over to the central crease.

3

Unfold the folds you made in step 2.

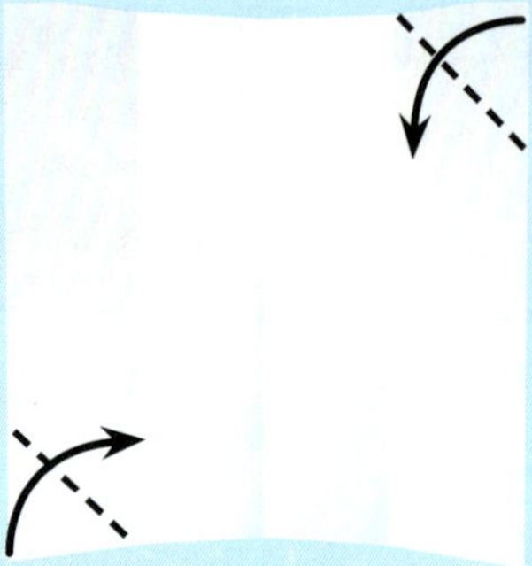

4

Valley fold the bottom left and top right corners over to the crease lines you made in step 2.

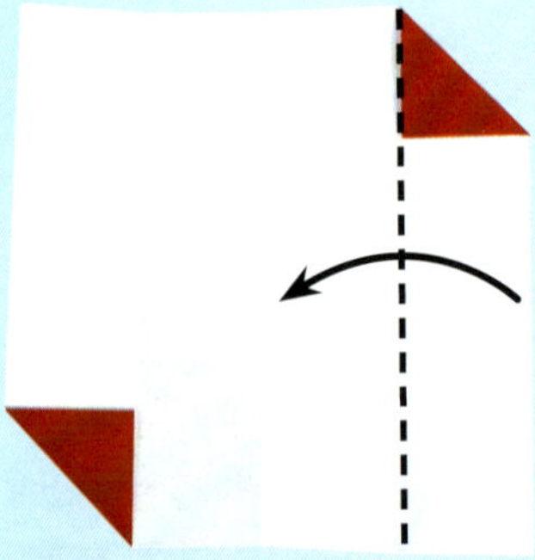

5

Refold the right-hand fold you made in step 2. Fold the paper over the triangle-shaped flap you made in step 4.

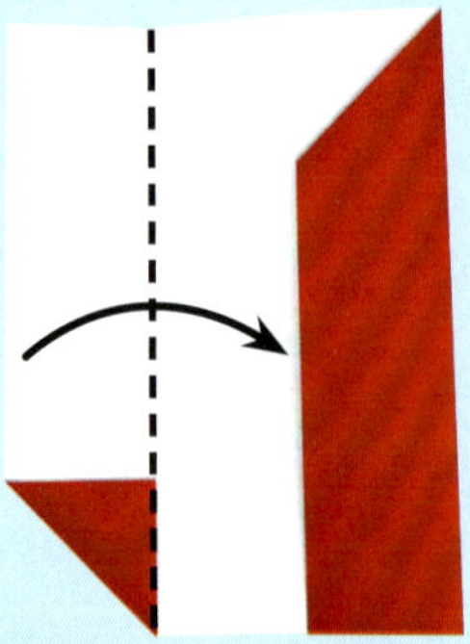

6

Repeat step 5 on the left-hand side.

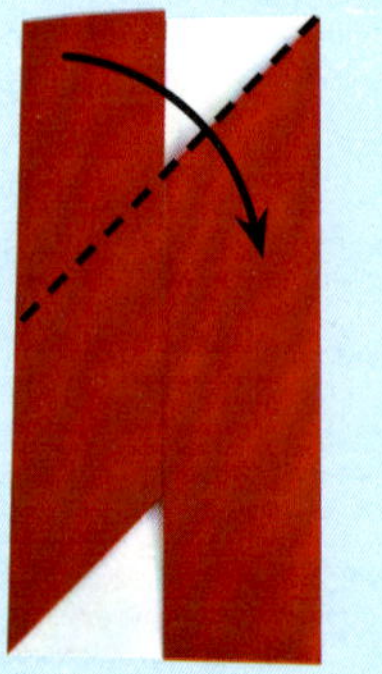

7

Fold the top left point down and to the right, so it lines up with the right-hand edge.

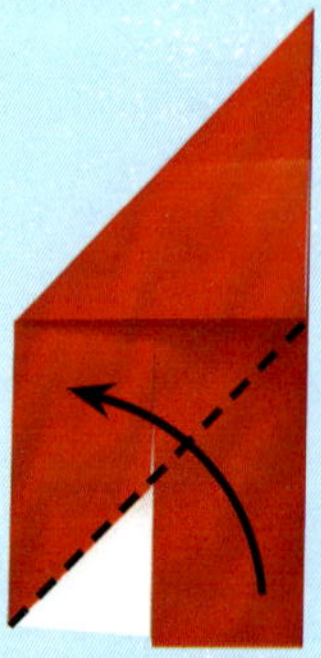

8

Now fold the bottom right point up and to the left, so it lines up with the left-hand edge.

Hard

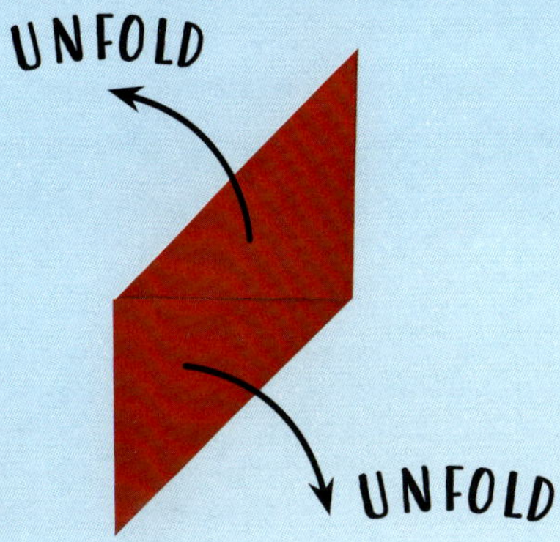

9

Unfold the folds you made in steps 7 and 8.

10

Take the top left point and fold it back over to the right edge, this time tucking it under the flap you made in step 5.

11

Tuck the point right under the flap and flatten it down.

12

Your paper should look like this. Now do the same with the bottom right point. Fold it back over to the left edge, tucking it under the flap you made in step 6.

13

Tuck the point right under the flap and flatten it down.

14

Your paper should look like this. Turn it over from left to right.

15

Rotate the paper 45° to the right.

16

Valley fold the top point down as shown.

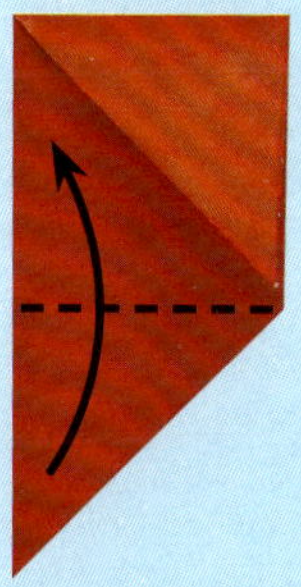

17

Valley fold the bottom point up.

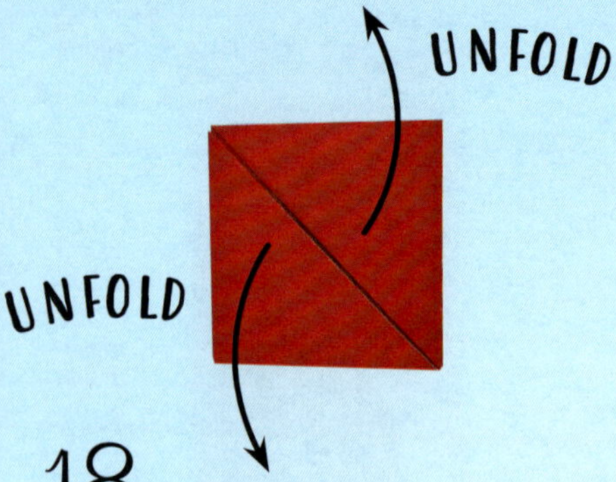

18

Unfold the folds you made in steps 16 and 17 part of the way, so the ends stick up toward you.

19

Your paper should look like this. Take the other two pieces of paper and repeat steps 1 to 18 with each, so you have three pieces folded the exact same way.

20

Take two of your pieces and position them like this. Slide the right-hand point of the left piece (red) inside the right piece (pink).

21

Keep pushing until it's all the way in.

22

Your pieces should look like this. Get your third piece and position it as shown.

23

Slide the point of the right (purple) piece into the other slot in the bottom of the pink piece, as shown, and keep pushing until it's all the way in.

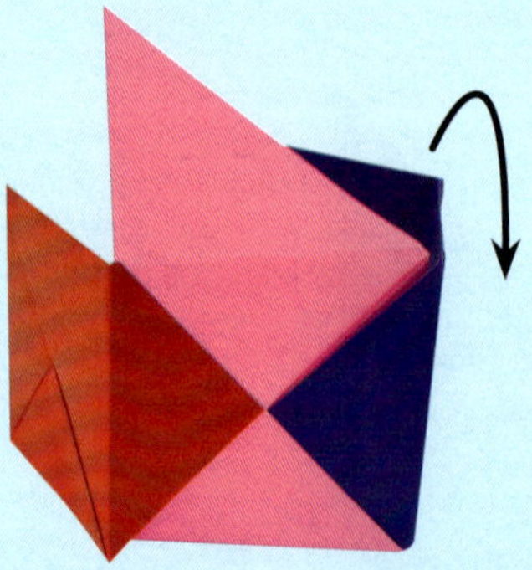

24

Turn all three pieces over, so the pink piece is lying flat, as shown in step 25.

25

Take the top point of the red triangle and bring it down to touch the right corner of the pink piece. It twists the red piece slightly.

Hard

26

While holding the red piece in position, bring the top point of the purple piece over and tuck it inside the far flap of the red piece.

27

Tuck it all the way in. The piece may bend or crumple a little, but you can straighten it out gently when it's fully tucked in.

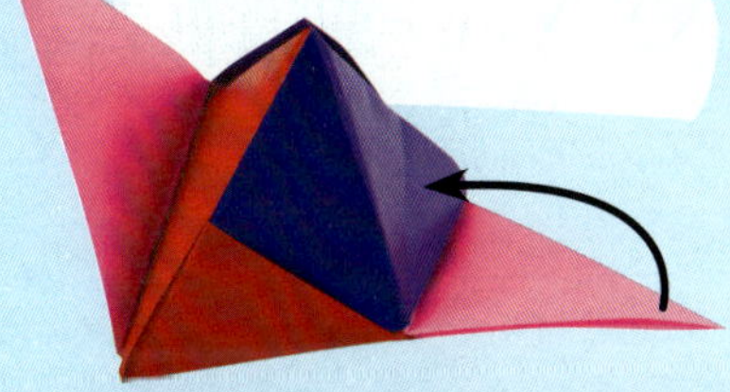

28

Your paper should look like this. Fold the point nearest to you (from the central pink piece) into the nearest purple flap.

29

Tuck it right in.

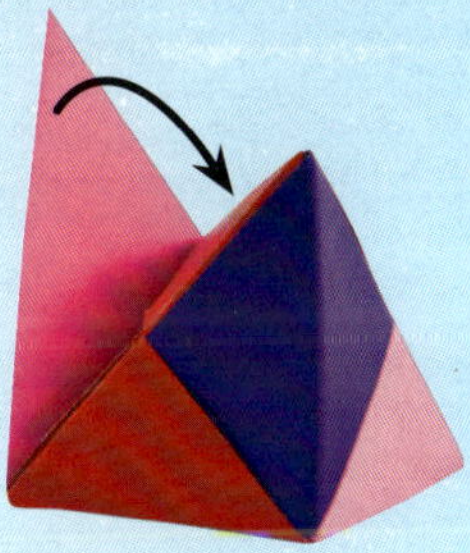

30

Fold the remaining pink point into the remaining red flap.

31

Push it right in.

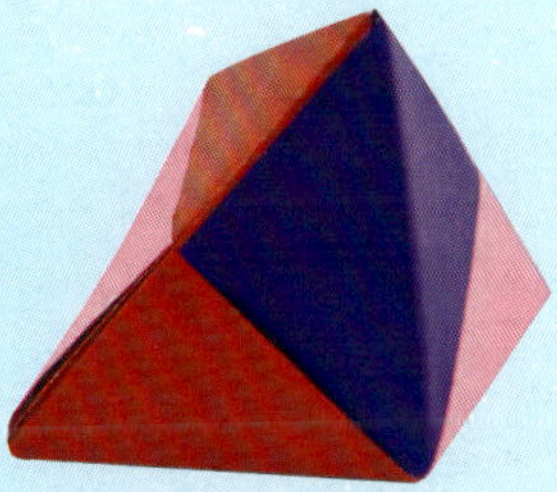

32

Your paper should look like this. Make sure all the flaps are tightly tucked, then position your jewel so it looks like the image in step 33.

33

Your jewel is ready. Why not fold some more to create your own treasure chest?

Magic Bracelet

This bracelet may be filled with magic. Once it's made, give it a quick rub and make a wish—it may just come true! You'll need scissors to complete this project.

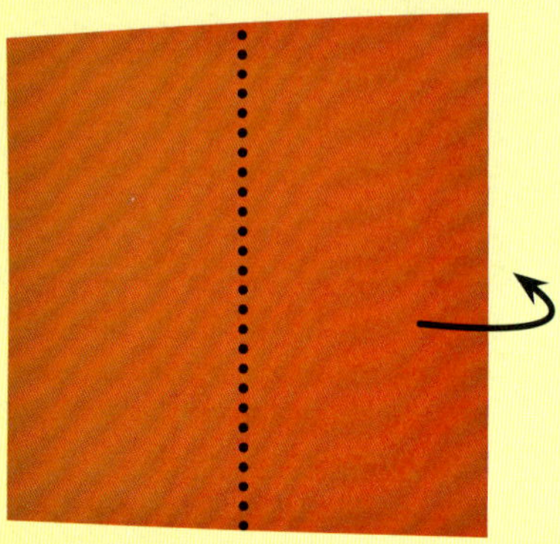

1

Place your paper like this, white side down, with a straight edge facing you. Mountain fold it in half from right to left, then unfold.

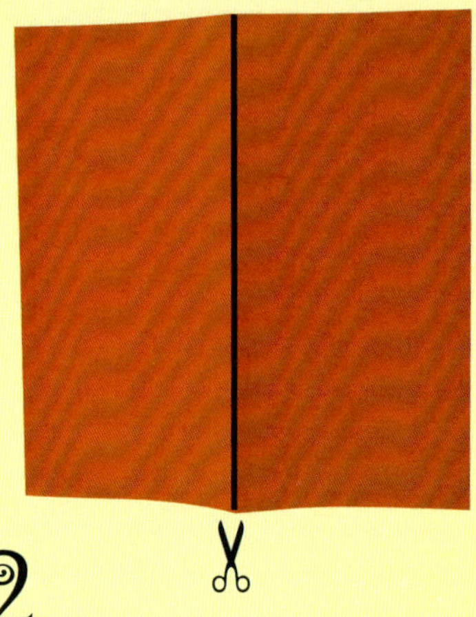

2

Carefully cut the paper in half along the fold line you made in step 1.

3

Take one of the pieces of paper and turn it over from left to right.

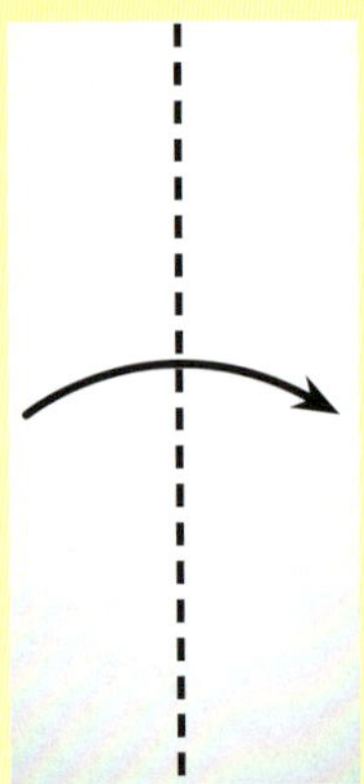

4

Valley fold it in half from left to right, then unfold.

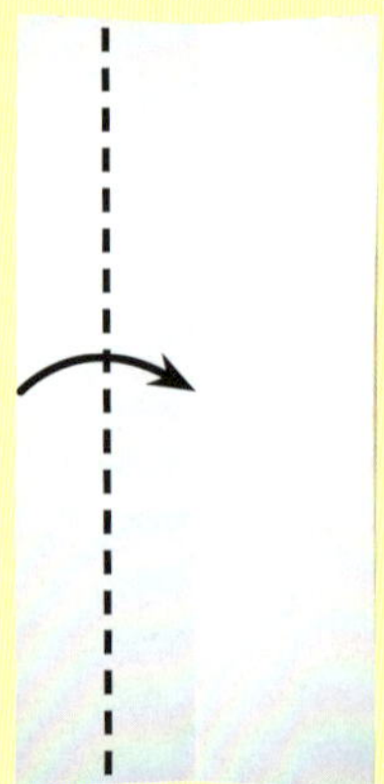

5

Valley fold the left-hand edge over to the central crease.

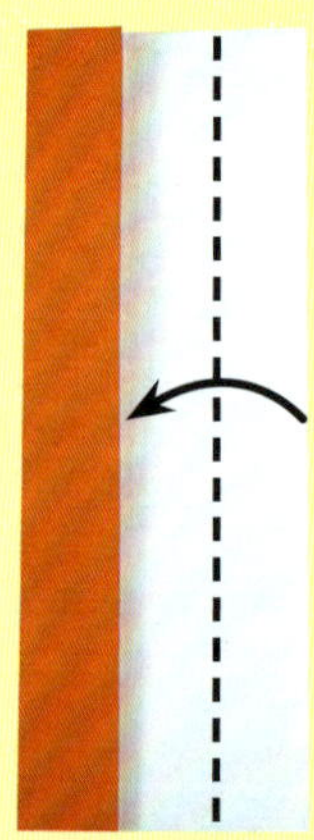

6

Repeat step 5 on the right-hand side.

Medium

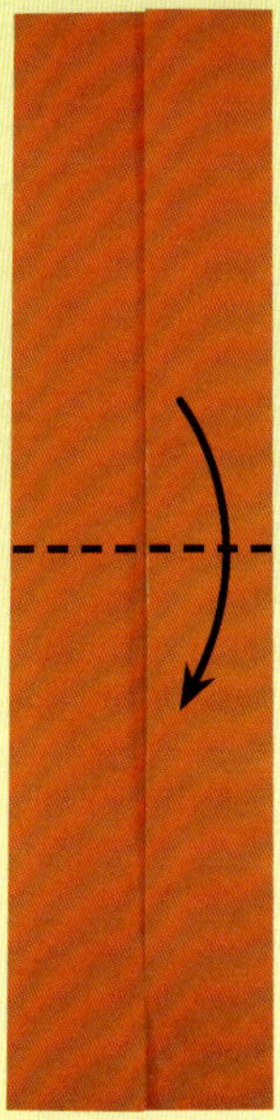

7
Your paper should look like this. Valley fold it in half from top to bottom.

8
Valley fold the top left corner over to the central crease.

9
Fold it the other way so it's also a mountain fold, then turn it into an inside reverse fold (see page 6).

10
Flatten the paper down.

11
Repeat steps 8 to 10 on the right-hand side.

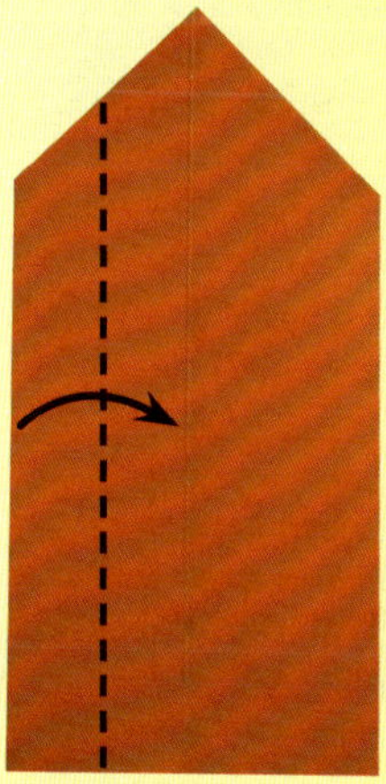

12
Valley fold the left-hand edge of the upper layer over to the central crease.

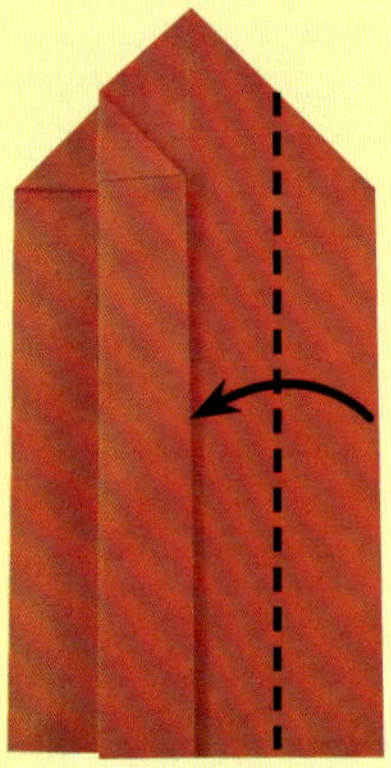

13

Repeat step 12 on the right-hand side.

14

Your paper should look like this. Turn it over from left to right.

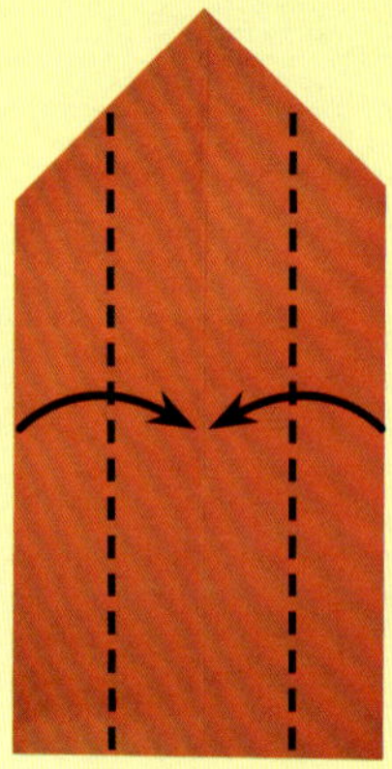

15

Now repeat steps 12 and 13 on this side.

16

Rotate the paper 90° to the right.

17

Unfold the bottom layer of the paper over to the right. As you do, the middle of the paper should form a pointed, crown-like shape pointing up toward you.

18

Lift the middle section of the paper up slightly.

19

Put your finger inside the middle section and push out the folds so they form a cube-like shape.

Medium

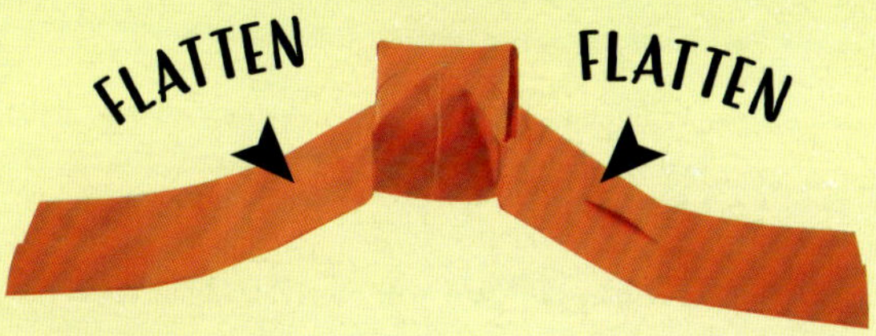

20
Your paper should look like this. Flatten down the flaps on either side again.

21
Rotate the paper 90° to the left.

22
Turn the paper over a quarter turn from right to left.

23
Curl the bands around to form your bracelet.

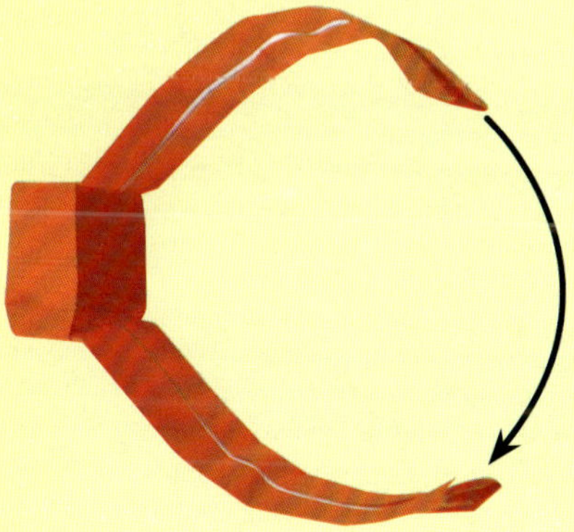

24
Fit one band inside the other.

25
Fasten the ends securely. You can use tape if you want.

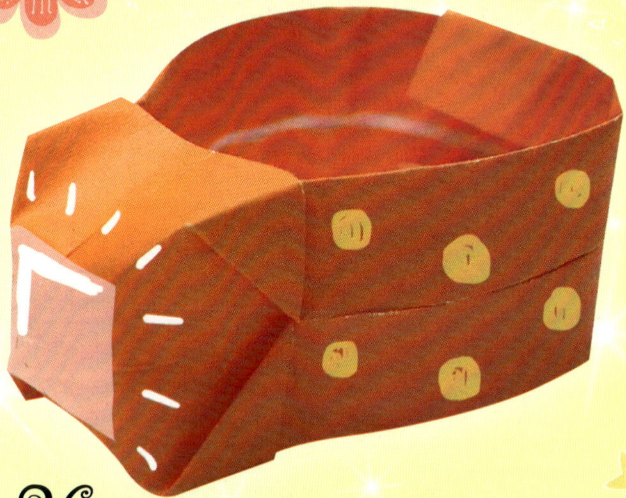

26
Your bracelet is ready. Decorate it with glittery paint to bring out the magic!

Glossary

CREASE A line made by a fold.

DIAGONAL A line in a sloping direction, from one corner to another.

KITE BASE A starting shape that looks like a kite.

MOUNTAIN FOLD A fold where the crease points up, like a mountain.

STEP FOLD A fold that creates a zigzag, or step, in the paper.

VALLEY FOLD A fold where the crease points away from you, like a valley.

Further Information

James, Elizabeth. *Easy Origami for Children.* Twickenham, UK: Kyle Craig Publishing, 2017.

Montroll, John. *Dragons and Other Fantastic Creatures in Origami.* Mineola, NY: Dover Publications, 2014.

Stephen, Ella. *Origami for Kids.* Independently published, 2019.

Top That Publishing. *Fold Your Own Fantastic Fairytale Unicorns.* Woodbridge, UK: Top That Publishing, 2019.

Index